The Great H̶a̶n̶n̶i̶b̶a̶l̶ ̶W̶a̶r̶s̶

The following work of fiction contains characters, events, and situations that are entirely products of the author's imagination. Any resemblance to actual persons, living or dead, or real events is purely coincidental. This book is a work of fiction and should be interpreted as such.

Copyright © John Barstin 2024

Communications to:
Photer, Inc.
PO Box 2215
Leesburg, VA 20177

ISBN 978-0-9740264-1-1
Printed in the United States of America
May 2024

Acknowledgement:

I want to thank my friends at Photer, Inc. for their support in the production and distribution of this book. I wish them all the best with their photo and travel app. Here's where you can find Photer:

Note from the Author:

This book was written in honor of the men and woman who serve or have served in the armed forces; especially to those, and the families of those, who have made the ultimate sacrifice. We owe a particular debt of gratitude to the greatest generation who fought in World War II. They put our country first to preserve our freedom and we should honor them with a similar commitment to each other and this great country.

My goal was to answer the question: How did America become so divided? The story highlights the causes of our division and offers suggestions on how to fix things. The solution begins with the fundamentals where we put country before party; fact before ideology; and civility above everything else. We can rebuild trust in each other and restore functional governance of a country that will remain indivisible with liberty and justice for all.

John Barstin

A friendly gathering

It was a cloudy September morning in Seattle. A group of old friends met for breakfast. Each year they volunteered to support a local children's charity run, and this gathering was to coordinate their efforts. They were seated at a long rectangular table inside a restaurant, and following their committee work, the discussion quickly turned to politics.

Susan, who arranged the meeting said, "I can't believe what's happening today. Politics is everywhere. I go online and see an interesting picture, read some of the comments, and the next thing you know it gets political. Comments start flying and then it gets ugly."

"I'm seeing this too," Marty confirmed. "It's gotten to the point where friendships have been interrupted, even some of my longest. And when I meet someone new, I look for clues to their politics. It's just not worth connecting with people who have different views. I don't want to let them in my friends' group or I'll have to avoid conversations as it just leads to arguments."

No one seemed surprised by Marty's statement.

"I'm worried where all this is headed," Susan said.

"Me too," Terrance agreed. "It's like there are two teams Republicans and Democrats. You're either on one or the other and everybody's fighting." It's not rational. It's purely emotional. Choose a side and hate the other."

Then, Steve said, "We're divided. We don't trust each other. We don't like each other. And what's really scary to me is that we don't even agree on the problems anymore." Heads nodded.

"How can we solve anything when we don't agree on the problems, or whether there's even a problem at all," Susan added.

Bill said, "You make it seem like there's only small differences."

"What do you mean?" Mark asked.

"We had an insurrection and half the public doesn't seem to care?" Bill answered.

"That's ridiculous," Tom said. "That's just because the media is constantly painting January 6th as the worst thing ever, while conveniently forgetting about all the destruction caused by Black Lives Matter (BLM) protests!"

Bill responded, "Oh, there you go again deflecting things. Can't you see that comparing the two is just a way to downplay the severity of the Capitol attack?"

Tom continued, "Don't you see the hypocrisy in only caring about violence when it fits your woke narrative? You're just using the Capitol attack to push your agenda!"

"Keep telling yourself that story," Bill said. "You're excusing domestic terrorists! You're blind to reality, living in your racist bubble!"

"Racist bubble? That's rich coming from someone who thinks violence is justified as long as it's for a so-called noble cause!"

"At least I'm aware of systematic racism," Bill stated.

"That's it, I'm done! I can't talk to someone who's this woke."

"Fine by me! I'd rather be woke than ignorant and racist like you!"

Then Tom stood up, tossed a twenty-dollar bill on the table, and stormed off in anger, ending the conversation abruptly.

Everyone was stunned and looked at each other in disbelief. Bill looked embarrassed and said, "I'm sorry we got into it like that."

"Well, this isn't the first time you've butted heads" John said. "Seems like every time we're together you guys are bickering. You need to avoid politics or you're going to lose friends."

"You're right," Bill replied as he looked around at all the shocked faces. "Again, I'm sorry."

"You're not the only ones arguing these days, and we have another election coming," John said. "It will likely get worse."

Marty said, "I have a friend who's trying to do something about it. He's written a story about the battle in America today with some thoughts on how to fix it."

"How can you explain this mess in a story?" Terrance asked. "It's too complicated."

"I felt the same way as you. But it will surprise you. It's about a world that becomes desperately divided. Does this sound familiar? Marty asked rhetorically. "Well, it made an impact on me and several of my friends. It's written in a straightforward manner and the characters and events are symbolic of the challenges we face today."

"Tell us about the character," Terrance said.

"There are six of them. There's a Wizard and an Oracle who represent science and religion. Two politicians - one from each of the major parties. And two broadcasters with opposing views."

"Sounds interesting," Susan said. "What's the title?"

"The Great Pickleball Wars." There were smiles all around and even a few chuckles.

"You've got me hooked," Terrance said.

"How about telling us the story? Linda asked.

"Sure," Marty said. "It's not that long. Let me get another cup of coffee and then I'll share it with you."

Then he refilled his cup from the carafe on the table and began.

The Story

Once, a long time ago, in a Universe far away, there was a tiny planet named Photer whose existence was threatened. Their sun was dying, energy was scarce and things were desperate.

Photer had four countries Struggle, Trouble, Dire, and Thrive. In earlier days, each country had vast blue oceans, rich green forests, and fertile soil. In the countryside the natives planted crops and raised livestock. In urban areas they had lots of manufacturing with plenty of parkland set aside for recreation.

One day, calamity struck. The sun exploded, and it was reduced to one third its original size. The blast left Photer intact, though radiation showered the entire planet. Photer's days were shorter, daylight was dim, and people could no longer bear children because of the radiation from the explosion. Within a few months things were becoming hopeless and even lawless. Lots of citizens had guns for self-protection, yet as things deteriorated, guns were used increasingly for crime, including mass shootings from those who had simply lost their sanity.

All was not lost for the tiny planet, as the Great Power of the Universe was aware of the situation and intervened to save it. The energy crisis was solved, violence subsided, and there was a new method for childbirth so life could continue.

The improvement occurred after the Great Power delivered the two Great Books. The Book of Faith was brought by an Oracle to offer spiritual guidance. The Book of Knowledge was provided by a Wizard to reveal scientific wonders. The Great Books were complex, often contradictory, and required lots of interpretation.

The mystics who brought them were very powerful, though they were generally not seen, and rarely interacted with people. Over time, many on Photer questioned whether they were even real. Together the mystics provide a deeper look into their world, revealing clues and some universal truths that may help us today!

The solution to the energy crisis was found within the pages of the Great Books. The Book of Faith contained clues that led to the discovery of special minerals that were the key to power generation. The Book of Knowledge revealed how to use the minerals to create a unique compound that could generate power. The book also highlighted the best methods for generating electricity, with the most efficient being the sports of tennis and pickleball. These became the primary activities on Photer. The compound was rapidly manufactured in large quantities and spread across their parklands. Immense power grids were created to store and transmit electricity to supply the world.

Before sending the books, The Great Power's first act addressed the lawlessness. He transformed all handguns into pickleball paddles and all rifles into tennis rackets to reduce the violence. As a result, there was plenty of sports gear available to support the activities that generated power.

The Great Power's second act brought tennis balls and pickleballs to life and gave them the ability to procreate, lay eggs, and repopulate the world. When pickleball eggs hatched, they either bore children or pickleballs and they were of various colors. Most were yellow, some orange, and a limited amount of blue; even the people. Similarly, when tennis ball eggs hatched, they bore children or tennis balls. Most of them were yellow in color as well, though some were orange or pink. As it turned out, people tended to congregate with people of the same color, except when playing sports, where it didn't seem to matter.

To be clear, pickleballs and tennis balls are from different species; like cats and dogs. And in the rare event when pickleballs and tennis balls procreated, the outcomes were square eggs. These were considered non-viable. If these eggs hatched, the life produced was generally limited to a vegetative state and rarely lived more than a few years. However, this revealed an absolute contradiction in the Great Books. The Book of Faith taught that all life was precious and was to be preserved, even those born from square eggs. Where the Book of Knowledge provided a method of *eggselection* to medically eliminate them.

Another contradiction in the Great Books was rackets and paddles. They were just sports equipment until people found ways to turn them back into weapons. The Book of Faith provided for the right to self-defense and protection of property. The Book of Knowledge spoke of the need for limitations as a means for safety, which was termed *racket control*.

Each country was governed by an elected Congress. Not surprisingly, the political systems revolved around pickleball and tennis. Laws were passed to regulate the games, the number and types of courts, *eggselection* and *racket control*.

The Congress of each of the countries were identical, with a Senate, a House of Representatives, a President, and a Judicial system. There were two Senators elected from each of the states with representatives elected from geographic voting districts that were based upon the population. Districts were determined by boundaries and were revised each decade after a census. Over time, two strong political parties emerged; the Tenniscans and the Picklecrats.

Media was simply called the *news* and it arrived in morning newspapers, evening television broadcasts, and weekly magazines. The news was presented factually and was regulated for fairness, balance, and truth.

In time, Photer recovered from its darkest days. Ecosystems flourished, the population grew, and technology expanded. All progress was inseparably linked to tennis and pickleball. On the surface things looked good, though underneath a political storm was brewing.

Almost 250 years passed since the explosion of the sun and the Great Power's intervention, but the planet is threatened anew. This time the threat comes from within. The people are extremely divided, and the four countries are each headed in different directions. The governments of Struggle and Trouble are barely functional. Dire is worse, as it is on the verge of civil war, and only Thrive seems to be healthy.

Division

The Wizard and the Oracle were determined to use their mystical power to help. Usually, they are very busy guiding the Universe and go their separate ways. Though, from time to time they met to discuss important matters such as the one at hand. So, they met in Dire to discuss the challenges its people are facing.

Their appearance is quite ordinary. The Oracle, named Hope, reveals herself as a young woman with a kind face and long flowing hair. She is warm, welcoming, and compassionate. She is steadfast in her beliefs and guided by a moral compass. The Wizard, named Professor, is a tall, thin, aged man with a scholarly face and professional demeanor. He is unemotional, a bit cold and dispassionate. He is exacting in manner and focused on the assessment of evidence and related outcomes.

Today they met at a little café across the street from Trembly Park, a major pickleball center. They have already ordered their coffee and are seated at a table near a window. Their conversation began.

"It's been a while," said Hope as she stirred her coffee.

"Time flies," Professor replied. "Glad we could connect."

"It's nice to see you, though these sure are trying times," Hope said. "And Dire is a powder keg," she continued.

"So, how did this happen?" Professor asked.

"One word; division," Hope replied. "And, everybody is arguing."

"Perhaps the answers can be found in the Great Books," Professor offered.

"That's part of the problem," Hope replied. "Folks are even arguing about them," she continued. They are confused. Some follow The Book of Faith and others follow The Book of Knowledge; as if they can be separated. But there's a lot more to it than that."

"This doesn't make sense to me as both of these books are from the Great Power," Professor said with a look of disbelief.

"People from rural areas follow The Book of Faith, and people from urban areas follow The Book of Knowledge," Hope explained, "and I do recognize that there are two major issues that have sparked the division."

This is true, as it is well known that The Book of Faith has pronouncements that are pro-egg, and The Book of

Knowledge provides the science and medical process for *eggselection*. Also, The Book of Faith is pro-rackets and provides for the right to self-defense and protection of property. The Book of Knowledge speaks to the need for limitations on weapons as a means for safety, which the people have now termed, *racket control*. Each of these moral issues have created big problems across Photer.

"Division occurs when there are absolutes," Professor said. "When things are all or nothing; black or white with no room for gray" he continued.

"And The Great Books are for guidance," Hope said. "Still, caution and compromise are essential when they are used for establishing laws and community rights."

"It's more complicated than just the differences between faith and knowledge," Professor explained. "You have to understand the lifestyle differences that I've observed."

Professor was correct. Rural areas tended to be conservative farming communities. Its people more religiously based with plenty of room for tennis courts. Urban areas are more crowded and tended to be liberal. It's where most of the colleges had been built that support scientific and medical pursuits. And, with the limited amount of space, it's generally better suited for pickleball.

"These differences have created a culture clash of pickleball vs. tennis," Professor concluded. This is reflected in the political contrast between Picklecrats and Tenniscans. On the one side there are Picklecrats who are urban, Book of Knowledge, *pro-eggselection*, and want *racket control*. On the other side there are Tenniscans who are rural, Book of Faith, *pro-egg*, and *pro-rackets*."

"So, you're saying the cause of their problems is pickleball and tennis?" Hope quipped.

"Not quite," Professor responded. "There are plenty of centrists who play both, but their influence is limited. The real cause is the two-party system, which has evolved into an environment of *us vs. them*," Professor stated emphatically. "These folks are no longer of one country, but two political teams, each tied ideologically to either pickleball or tennis."

"How did the teams get so entrenched?" Hope asked.

"Gerrymandering," Professor answered.

Professor explained that every ten years new voting districts are established across each of the countries. It begins with a census, with states being awarded their share of voting districts based on population. The lines for voting districts are drawn by each of the state legislatures. And, when the party that controls the state legislature slants the districts to favor their political party, it's called Gerrymandering.

"At first Gerrymandering was used by the parties to concentrate populations into districts that favored either Picklecrats or Tenniscans, which created safe districts that protected incumbents," Professor said. "And over time, the party in charge drew the lines to further their party's political advantage."

Professor described that as the number of super concentrated districts grew, so did the number of extreme representatives, who are less willing to compromise. This created greater division between the parties and now even within the parties.

"How do you know so much about this?" Hope asked.

"I watch their news. They seem to fight about this all the time and their court systems are regularly involved in settling disputes on how to draw the district lines," Professor said.

He continued to explain that with the larger number of safe districts, the parties focused their time and money on the competitive ones making campaigns in these districts more expensive. Primary voters are generally aligned with the party's traditional position on major issues. This helps to reinforce the party line with politicians who may have different views.

"It sounds like they've made it nearly impossible for outsiders to get elected," Hope said.

"Exactly," Professor replied. "And as for incumbents, they need to follow the party ideology or they'll get *Primaried*; meaning the party will back a challenger. That's why I blame the two-party system for the gridlock. And there's more," Professor continued.

Just then, they were interrupted by a man with a clipboard.

"Excuse me," the man said. "Are you aware there's an election next week," he asked? The man explained that he lived in the neighborhood and the issue that he wanted us to support was the need to change the voting rules.

"What change is being considered?" Hope asked.

The man answered, "The size of the majority required to make changes to land use rules. Presently, it takes a two-thirds majority to change these rules and that makes it hard to develop property. So, as a practical matter, we'd like to make things easier for things to progress by requiring only a simple majority. This will allow us to improve our community."

This seemed a bit odd to Hope. She shrugged her shoulders and said, "We don't live here, but let me ask you a question. Does this have anything to do with pickleball?"

After a pause, the man answered quietly, "Why yes. There's a group of us who wants to add more pickleball courts on some vacant land, and also to convert some of the unused tennis courts to pickleball courts."

Then, from across the room came a shout. "You hear that," yelled a man to his companion. He was clearly a Tenniscan and he wanted everyone to know it. As he was wearing the party's symbolic yellow hat, representing the majority color of tennis balls. "Damn Picklecrats! Not only do they want to steal our tennis courts, they want to make us pay for theirs!"

"Yes, I'm a Picklecrat, but it's not like that," the man with the clipboard responded.

"Don't be fooled by this guy," the man in the yellow hat demanded. His face was red with anger as he got up, and he headed towards the entrance and ripped down a flyer. "Here, take a look at this," he insisted as he handed it to Hope.

Hope looked at it quickly and read the headline out loud. "New Pickleball Cluster…. is a Cluster!" And continued, "It will get even worse with the conversion of three tennis courts to six pickleball courts."

Then she paraphrased the rest of it. "Looks like folks are worried about all the noise, the bullying of their children, and even public urination. And it ends: Do you want more of this?" Hope relayed.

Then the man in the yellow hat interrupted them. "First, they take our rackets. Then they take our eggs.   And now they want to take away our voting rights. Well, they're not going to take our tennis courts too! We'll fight for them!"

"That's not true," the man with the clipboard retorted.

It's the Tenniscans who are trying to control things. They're a minority. Their numbers are declining yet they have fixed things so they control the legislature and the town council. They're science deniers, *anti-eggselection*, and their rackets are killing our children."

Hope interrupted them. "There's got to be a better way to work through these things," she insisted.
"I don't think so," the man with the clipboard said.
"There's going to be a civil war."

"Finally, we agree on something," the man with the yellow hat responded. "Although, as I see it, The Great Pickleball Wars have already begun!"

Hope and Professor looked at each other with resolve. They had heard enough and stopped everything, even time. You see, the mystics had tremendous power. Though to use it, they had to work together and coordinate their efforts. This was one of those rare occasions.

If there's going to be a civil war, then there has to be two sides," Professor said. And the two sides in this war are Tenniscans and Picklecrats," he said without equivocation.

"So, you are blaming the two parties." Hope stated.

"Yes." Professor answered. "Though, it's bigger than just two parties, it's the two-party system that's driving this."

"We need to haul in their political leaders and get to the bottom of it," Hope insisted.

Professor said, "Let me do some research first." And he closed his eyes and used his power to review information throughout all time. He could visualize all the news accounts of Photer's political system in his head. After several minutes, he exclaimed, "I've got it. I can make sense of this."

"Well enlighten me," Hope requested.

"It's a bit complicated," Professor said. "But, I'll give it a try."

He explained that the main function of the House is to initiate the annual budget process and the Senate's job is to review and approve appointments of the President. Then he continued that the parties seemed to be oriented around two moral issues that dominate their elections: *eggselection* and *racket control*.

"You see," Professor said, "I've discovered that they have two teams fighting for control. When one party is in charge, the other party doesn't want them to accomplish anything. Otherwise, they'll get credit which may help them win more seats and further strengthen their party's power at the expense of the other."

Hope said, "But you said their job is to run things on behalf of the country. Right?"

"I thought so," Professor answered. "Now, I'm not so sure. Instead of working together, the parties obstruct each other by filibustering appointments and blocking budgets," Professor continued.

"How does a country operate without a budget?" Hope asked.

"Not very well," Professor answered sternly.

Hope asked rhetorically, "So what you're telling me, is that politicians get elected on the moral issues of *eggselection* and *racket control*, yet their job is to direct spending and oversee leadership appointments made by the President? And when their party isn't in charge their mission is to obstruct the other party from getting anything done?"

"You got it," Professor answered.

"That's crazy," Hope insisted. "Perhaps they simply don't know what they're doing," she speculated.

"No," Professor replied. "They know exactly what they're doing. Most of them have been there so long that they've figured out how to *not* work together," he said with disgust.

Then Professor rattled off a bunch of statistics:
- 90% seek re-election
- 95% of those win re-election
- 10 years is the average tenure in the House
- 12 years is the average tenure in the Senate
- Greater than 50% have served over 10 years

- Graduation rate from House to Senate is 50%
- Senators with House experience have already served 10 years in the House
- Senators with House experience have a combined tenure over 25 years

It was evident that the days of citizen legislators on Struggle and Trouble were long gone. Each had a divided government with one party in control of the Senate and the other controlling the House. Struggle has a Picklecrat President and Senate, and a Tenniscan House. Trouble has a Tenniscan President and House, with a Picklecrat Senate.

Professor said, "The governments on Struggle and Trouble are hopelessly stuck. Budgets, judges, legislation - everything is obstructed. They refer to this as loyal opposition."

"Well, let's investigate this so-called loyal opposition and see if they can explain it," Hope suggested.

Professor agreed and together they used their power and poof... Struggle's Tenniscan House leader and Trouble's Picklecrat Senate leader magically appeared.

The Politicians

The politicians arrived in an area that looked like a courtroom. They were seated directly in front of the mystics who were elevated slightly above them. It was smokey, and the room had an eerie feel. The smoke was from truth serum that the mystics used with their guests so they could get the facts. The politicians were confused. Then Hope oriented them on how they got here and the purpose of their visit.

"Who are you?" Tenniscan asked.

"I am the Oracle and my name is Hope, and this is the Wizard and his name is Professor."

"I didn't think you were real," Picklecrat said nervously.

"Oh, we are very real, and we're here to help you" Hope said gently.

"So you're here to help us?" Tenniscan asked skeptically. "Are we on trial? If so, what are the charges?"

"No," Hope answered. "You're not on trial. We're simply trying to understand the politics and the governments on Struggle and Trouble. We have observed your political systems and have brought you here to explain it to us."

Professor said, "specifically, we want to understand the gridlock and how you've gotten so divided."

Tenniscan had an automatic reply as if he was responding to a reporter. "I recognize your concern," he began. "There are challenges to bipartisan collaboration and differences in our policy priorities and ideological perspectives. Clearly, we need to be open to dialogue to find common ground. Though, I am optimistic for our future cooperation. And that we can bridge these gaps to find areas of consensus despite our current tensions."

Picklecrat added similarly, "I agree with my distinguished colleague. I too am optimistic about our future. Though, we have some very real differences, like the role of government, taxation, spending priorities, and individual rights like *eggselection* and *racket control*."

"Then why are you obstructing each other rather than working together?" Hope asked pointedly.

"It's our duty as elected officials to represent the interests of our constituents," Picklecrat answered. "When we oppose certain legislation, it's because we believe it doesn't align with the best interests of the people, not simply to obstruct. We are wide open to discussion to work through the issues."

"Likewise," Tenniscan interjected. "We're always open to bipartisan discussion. In fact, there have been several instances recently where we've reached across the aisle. However, it's essential that these discussions are based on mutual respect and a genuine interest in finding common ground. Still, we won't compromise our principals just for the sake of appearing cooperative."

Professor continued his line of questioning. "Don't you think that there's a difference between legitimate policy disagreements and refusing to cooperate or engage in bipartisan action?" Professor asked.

"To us, things seem broken," Hope added. "And worse, you're polarized."

"Polarization is a concern," Tenniscan answered. "And it's not just on one side. Both parties have played a role in the current state of the union. That said, I believe in leading by example. We're constantly reaching out, proposing amendments, and looking for ways to collaborate. But, it's a two-way street. Both sides need to come to the table and be willing to work together."

Professor directed his next question to Picklecrat. "So, tell me, what's your vision for a more collaborative and productive Congress?"

"A collaborative Congress begins with open dialogue," Pickelcrat answered. "We need to prioritize listening to each other and finding those areas where we can agree. There's more that unites us than divides us. It's about putting country over party and focusing on the issues that truly matter to the people. I just wish Tenniscans would listen more."

"It's not that we aren't listening. On Struggle, we just out vote you," Tenniscan said with a chuckle.

Professor nodded his head with disapproval and stared in disbelief at Hope.

"Spoken like true politicians," Professor stated sharply.

"Even with truth serum these guys can't be straight with us," Hope offered sadly.

"Let's increase the dosage," Professor snickered.

The smoke got thicker in the room as more truth serum was added. Hope and Professor were clearly dissatisfied with the conversation thus far. Obstructionism was rampant in both Struggle and Trouble and the politicians seemed totally comfortable with this. Neither Congress had passed a budget on time in the past six years. In fact, together they have only passed 3 budgets on time in the past forty years. There was no significant progress on domestic issues for decades, including immigration. During that time, the use of filibusters as a legislative stall tactic has gone from rarely used to almost daily. Struggle's Picklecrat Senate minority blocked 30 judicial appointments with 14 withdrawn this year. Which was similar to the last time Tenniscans were the Senate minority as they blocked 35 judicial appointments with 12 withdrawn over a similar period.

"Why are you blocking judicial appointments?" Hope asked. "Don't you need judges for your system to function?"

"There are many issues where we have different philosophical approaches," Picklecrat said. "And the judiciary is one of them. We need to make sure that judges do not have a predisposition on issues that are important to our constituents."

"We agree," Tenniscan said. "Important decisions on *eggselection* and *racket control* can't be left to chance. We want judges who will decide these cases our way." If we don't block them, they will abolish *eggselection*," Picklecrat said.

Tenniscan laughed noticeably.

"Your laughing," Professor stated, directing his growing frustration towards Tenniscan.

"Yes," Tenniscan answered. "That's exactly what we are doing to them on Trouble. If we don't block them, they'll take away our rackets."

"Okay, then why block budgets?" Professor continued.

"We don't want to fund their socialist agenda" Tenniscan replied.

Picklecrat interjected, "And we don't want budgets that favor the interests of the wealthy and corporations over ordinary citizens by ignoring investment in public services and social programs.

Hope asked, "There are some areas in which you agree, so why not make progress?"

Tenniscan responded, "Progress is important when you're in charge, so your party gets the credit. Otherwise, if they win, we lose."

Picklecrat nodded his head in total agreement.

"Why not compromise?" Hope asked.

"There is no compromise on fundamental rights," Picklecrat said.

Tenniscan agreed and said, "Of course, if you do compromise, then your own party will turn on you and you won't get reelected."

"But what if you agree with the other side?" Professor asked. "Don't the parties allow you to vote your conscience?"

"No." Tenniscan and Picklecrat said in unison.

"The last few who did this got *primaried*," Picklecrat said fearfully.

"Remind me, what happens when you're *primaried*?" Hope asked.

"That's when an incumbent's own party or a special interest use their money to back another candidate in primary elections," Tenniscan answered.

"That's right. Go against your party and they'll show you no mercy. You'll be shot in the back by your own troops," Picklecrat added.

"So, you won't even consider compromising on *eggselection* or *racket control*?" Hope asked "Compromise on *eggselection* and *racket control*?" Tenniscan said with alarm.

Picklecrat laughed. "That's a good one," he said with a slur, as he put his arm around the shoulder of Tenniscan like they were drinking buddies at a bar. On this subject, they were brothers in arms as they continued to muse at the thought of bucking their parties and compromising; a bit punch drunk from the extra truth serum.

"So, you're blaming your parties for all of this?" Professor asked.

"Yes," they again answered in unison.

Professor seemed satisfied with their answer, as he had reached the same conclusion. Still, he was frustrated by their general sense of helplessness. He had expected more from them given their leadership roles.

"Don't you take any responsibility for this?" Professor jabbed.

"Well at least we're functioning. In Dire, they're on the verge of civil war," Picklecrat stated.

"And why do you think it's worse in Dire?" Hope asked.

"The media," Tenniscan answered.
"Money," Picklecrat answered.

They were both right. The parties were part of the problem and so were the media and money. The mystics had heard enough for now and again stopped everything. The politicians were frozen in place as Professor did a bit more research.

He closed his eyes and used his powers to review the relevant news accounts of the impact of media and money on Photer's political system. It did not take long and after a minute or so Professor stated, "That was easy."

"What have you discovered?" Hope asked.

"About 30 years ago the Federal Communication Commission in Dire stopped regulating the media and within a few years the other countries followed their lead. Prior to this, there were three broadcast networks each having an evening newscast with similar content. There was a fairness doctrine that required broadcast license holders to present controversial issues of public importance in a manner to fairly reflect differing viewpoints. The public was provided essentially the same story so there was no question about the facts. Now, without regulation, the networks were no longer required to separate news from editorial content, even fact from fiction," Professor said.

"That doesn't sound good," Hope said.

"It's not," Professor replied. "The lack of regulation allowed the number of media outlets to grow tremendously. It also changed the news cycle from morning newspaper, nightly TV news broadcast, and weekly magazines to a 24-hours a day, 7 days a week rhythm."

"Has this led to a well-informed public?" Hope asked.

"Yes and no. There's plenty of information. In fact, there's too much information. Trust me, I reviewed it all," Professor insisted with a grin. "But understanding it has become a major problem. Once the regulation stopped, the variety of news revealed a growing political bias, and the editorial content increased significantly. Currently in Dire, there is so much editorial content in the news that it's impossible to get the truth," Professor concluded.

"Can you show me some examples, so I can experience it for myself?" Hope asked.

"I have something in mind," Professor answered. "Let's bring in two of their popular broadcasters, the ones they call TV personalities, and we'll have a little chat."

The Media

There were many news networks in Dire. One was Pickleball News Network (PNN) considered a mainstream media outlet favored by Picklecrats. Another was Frank News favored by Tenniscans.

From PNN they brought in Snarky Matters who hosts an evening political commentary show watched by millions of Picklecrats. He is in his early 50's with black curly hair, round glasses, and a button-down shirt. Snarky is well educated and lets you know it. He is sarcastic and the type of person who likely sat in the front row in school and thought he was smarter than the teacher... and probably was.

From Frank News they brought in Jane Hostility, who similarly hosts an evening political commentary show watched by millions of Tenniscans. She is 30 something with silvery blonde hair and looks like a model. Hostility is a fierce debater, and seems angry. She was probably the "it girl" in high school and the mean sorority sister in college.

Time is suspended. Professor and Hope have summoned the two broadcasters to explain what is happening in Dire and specifically the role media has played. The broadcasters arrive from out of the blue and are given a dose of the smoky truth serum.

They are seated in the same room as the politicians. Though, the politicians have moved off to the side so they can only observe and are not allowed to speak. The broadcasters are confused at first and upon recognizing each other and the politicians began to ask questions. Hope calmed them down and informed them of the purpose of their visit. Then, Professor initiated the discussion with a question.

"As you know, Dire is on the verge of civil war. To what degree are you and the shows you host responsible for today's polarity?"

"Your question seems to have already reached its conclusion," Hostility stated. "Do you think the Media is to blame for it?" she asked.

"Well, isn't it?" Professor replied.

"You overestimate us," Hostility said. "Sure, each of us has a large following, but the cause of today's problems is not TV shows like ours. We're simply reporters; broadcasters of information."

"But your message is all about generating outrage," Professor countered.

"Look, we're in the editorial business and there's nothing wrong with sparking debate and engaging our viewers.

And our advertisers want to reach an engaged market, so I make no apologies for this," Hostility stated firmly.

"Are you saying that your message doesn't matter? That it's all about ratings without any responsibility for the content? Professor asked. "All you are doing is creating echo chambers."

"What's an echo chamber?" Hope asked.

Professor explained that an echo chamber is an environment where people only encounter information or opinions that reflect and reinforce their own. So, groups of like-minded people can become insular and build some very intense and at times misguided convictions when they aren't exposed to a broader view of opinions and information.

"Well, at least our news is factual," Snarky stated as he inserted himself into the conversation, looking at Hostility as he spoke.

"That's a lot of BS," Hostility responded. "The liberal mainstream media has been misleading the public for years with their biased view of the so-called news. You're totally editorial," she insisted.

"There you go, labeling me as a liberal," Snarky said. Your *alternate facts*, or lies, more simply stated, fuel one rightwing conspiracy theory after another. Where's the news value in that? All you do is confuse people and create an environment of distrust."

"We're not the only ones with conspiracy theories," Hostility replied, raising her voice in anger.

"Even worse is that you package it all with dog whistles and racist rhetoric," Snarky added.

"I am not a racist as you're insinuating, and I don't use that kind of language," Hostility stated emphatically.

"But your guests do, and you deliver it raw every day," Snarky said.

"That's called free speech," Hostility responded. "I let my guests present their thoughts. You Socialists are always trying to take away everybody's rights. You want to regulate what we can say, and how we can say it with all your political correctness. You're all a bunch of snowflakes," Hostility stated.

"Sure, you want free speech alright, except of course in books," Snarky countered. "Then under the guise of your religion you want to ban them. Talk about snowflakes. You prefer feel-good history to the truth. You're all a bunch of fascists!"

"Look, there's a troubling trend in our schools where some teachers seem to be instilling a sense of dislike of our country. We need to ensure that our education system promotes love for our country rather than fostering division. And quite frankly, you seem to be one of those who hates our country," Hostility said.

"Stop it!" Hope demanded. "I've heard enough of your sniping. It certainly didn't take long for the two of you to be at each other's throats," Hope said with a hint of sadness in her voice.

It wasn't the broadcasters arguing that was making Hope sad, rather it was what they represented. To her, they represented the many millions of people who were fighting over these very same issues.

After a pause, Hope continued. "Arguments like these are very common in Dire and both of you are part of the problem. It's all the labeling, the anger, and the distortion. You can be angry at real enemies, but villainizing your neighbors doesn't serve any purpose other than to create political division."

"We're just a drop in the bucket," Snarky offered. "We're nothing compared to the avalanche of lies and hate amplified by social media."

Hostility nodded her head in agreement.

Hope wondered aloud how it all worked? Professor, who had researched this, explained it to her. He emphasized that social media platforms collect and retain users' personal data and interests and over time they learn what keeps them engaged. It's essentially psychological profiling based on algorithms that recommend content with personalized delivery. This creates endless scrolling and a highly engaging experience. And it's all designed to keep users spending more and more time on the platform. This in turn supports an advertising business model whose value increases with size and engagement.

After Professor finished, Snarky interjected, "It's like drugs, and social media platforms are the pushers. Or perhaps, it's more like a trainwreck; you might not be searching for one, but when it shows up, you can't take your eyes off of it."

"That sounds terrible," Hope said.

"Well, it's not all trainwrecks," Snarky admitted, revising his comment. "Some folks like cats, or dogs, or travel, or sports. It's whatever engages you the most and it varies. But when it's political, that's when it goes off the rails."

"Finally, we agree on something" Hostility said. "I hate all those unsolicited posts, sponsored information and tons of fake comments from Bots."

"What are Bots?" Hope asked.

"Bots are something I discovered in my research," Professor offered.

Then Professor explained that Bots are computer generated users, who open automated accounts and often take on personas like real people. They can mimic human behavior and it's difficult to know that they are fake. Further, Bots can be employed by the thousands on social media to create trends that influence and manipulate the public.

Hope continued her line of questions, wondering why people couldn't tell what's true from what's fake. Professor explained that it was a slippery slope as users are initially shown content that aligns with their existing beliefs. Then through algorithms they are gradually exposed to sponsored content that is increasingly slanted or has extreme political views and over time can shift people politically from moderate to extreme and can even radicalize some.

Snarky added, "I get that it's a business to engage users and make money. Still, it's outrageous that it doesn't matter to them whether the information they are pushing is true or not. Sound familiar?" He added with a smirk and glared at Hostility.

"Get off your high horse, what you're peddling is worse," Hostility replied shaking her head with a disgusted expression on her face.

Hope raised her hand and motioned them to stop; reminding them to keep things civil.

The broadcasters relented.

"Okay, okay" Snarky said. "It's just frustrating to me that social media companies can get away with pushing this stuff to an unprotected public and nobody is doing anything about it."

Hope sympathized with him.

Professor seemed to agree and explained that it's coordinated. Sponsors pay social media companies to push political content. Bots then spread false narratives, amplify visibility, and shape public opinion, which can even effect election results.

"Who's paying for all of this?" Hope asked.

"That's the problem. It's invisible," Hostility said.

Professor continued to educate Hope on the subject. He explained that *Sponsors* are not just businesses advertising their goods, they include political campaigns, special interest groups, individuals, and political activists with their own agendas. Sponsored content is pushed by friend and foe; foreign and domestic. Further, the funds to pay for political material invisibly is called *dark money* as it is undisclosed and difficult to trace. He added that the lack of transparency makes it challenging for the public to identify and scrutinize the motives behind political messages that potentially sway public opinion without accountability.

"At least you know who's advertising on my show," Snarky offered.

"Oh really," Professor questioned. "I saw some of the advertisements during your shows. Tell me, who funds Citizens for a Better Tomorrow or Friends of Dire, and what are their motives?" He asked pointedly.

Snarky and Hostility were silent as they were fully aware that their sponsors used dark money on their shows.

Then Professor stated his conclusion. "Each of you is part of the problem. The combination of misinformation with unlimited amounts of dark money creates confusion and polarizes political views. And when it's reinforced anonymously through echo chambers it creates mistrust and division; which undermines the fabric of your democracy. That's what's happening in Dire today and their politicians are doing nothing to stop it," he added emphatically.

"We're screwed," Hostility said under her breath.

"Exactly," Snarky agreed.

"Not necessarily, but it may get worse, before it gets better," Hope offered.

"What do you mean?" Picklecrat asked.

"We'll show you," Hope answered.

The Future

Hope ushered the broadcasters and the politicians to the table where she and Professor were sitting.

"It's time for us to show you the future in Dire, Struggle, Trouble, and Thrive," Hope said. "Though the future revealed is based on the current path being taken by the people of each of the countries. Things can be different."

"We'll start with Dire, which is a warning of the looming civil war that you all may experience. Then we'll show you Struggle and Trouble to provide an example of the extremes when one party dominates the other and controls everything. Finally, we'll show you Thrive to demonstrate the resilience of democracy and reveal a guide to the possibilities. Remember, we don't control the choices that will be made nor the path that will be taken. It's up to the people, though we can encourage the braver angels among you to right the ship and work towards better days."

Professor began to describe what will happen in future Dire over the next fifteen years. "The anger and mistrust will continue to build. Its government will grow even more paralyzed and the people will lose faith. They'll lose faith in the voting process and each other. In five years, there will be an election that will be deadlocked, with twelve states fighting over its outcome. That's when the civil war begins."

Then Professor showed them holograms of newscasts from future Dire. "It's dreadful. It reveals how militias will be organized with violent skirmishes at state capitols as each side tries to control the results of the election. Within fifteen years battles like these are common and Dire will be engaged in a full-fledged civil war."

The viewers were motionless and sat in stunned silence.

After several minutes, Picklecrat asked, "how does it all end?"

"We don't know, it hasn't happened yet," Professor reminded them.

"I don't understand," Tenniscan said in a low voice.

"It can be changed," Hope reminded them. "The people of today have the freedom to make different choices."

"In what way?" Snarky asked.

"We'll show you. I'll give you a view of Struggle's future," Hope said.

"And, I'll show you future Trouble," Professor said.

Hope began, "In future Struggle, the gerrymandering continues and it significantly favors the Picklecrats to the point where they will control everything, the presidency, the House, and Senate. And with their super-majority they control the judiciary as well. This allows them to fully implement their agenda.

Picklecrat said, "That's what our party works towards and it sounds like a dream."

Professor followed, "Similarly, in future Struggle, the gerrymandering continues and it significantly favors the Tenniscans to the point where they will control everything, the presidency, the House, and Senate. And with their super-majority they control the judiciary as well. This allows them to fully implement their agenda.

Tenniscan said, "That's what our party works towards and it sounds like a dream to me as well."

The room goes dark except for two spotlights at the front of the room. Under the light on the far left is a woman and under the light on the far right is a man. They each look real but they are holograms.

The woman on the left begins, "I'm a teacher and I live in Liberty which is a typical small town in Struggle. I've been brought here to tell you what things are like living where everything is controlled by Tenniscans. Simply put, it's a nightmare.

The man on the right says, "I'm a small business owner and I live in Freedom which is a typical small town in Struggle. I've been brought here to tell you what things are like living where everything is controlled by Picklecrats. Simply put, it's a nightmare.

The woman continues, "Trouble is a police state. It's a totalitarian society where everyone is armed and they've locked up all the Picklecrat leaders. They've closed all the libraries and burned all the books. They've also closed the public schools to prevent what they call indoctrination and require that all children be either home schooled or attend approved religious institutions for their education. They've repealed all of the labor laws, and there's no minimum wage. The good news is that nobody is homeless. The bad news is that indentured servitude is now legal. Large corporations can house and feed their employees, debtor's prisons have been re-established, and being homeless is illegal. They've repealed all environmental protection laws so the water is polluted and the air is barely breathable. Welcome to Liberty, where you are free to live and pray their way."

The man then begins. He says, "Struggle is anarchy, it's a socialist society. They've taken all our rackets and ammunition and locked up all the Tenniscan leaders opposed to this tyranny. They've defunded the police and funded the schools to become totally responsible for raising all our children. The good news is that people are free to live and sleep where ever they please. The bad news is that open drug use is legal and the occupation of public space has led to the closing of most small businesses like mine. And we were the ones paying the taxes to support this mess. Equality is paramount, including wealth which has been redistributed. Income is similar as all work is deemed of equal value so everyone gets paid the same hourly wage. The environment is fully protected, but our jobs are not. So, unemployment is high, taxes are high, and healthcare is free. Though, it's not very good. Welcome to Freedom, where everything is free and everyone is equally free to live in squaller."

The group was silent. After a while, Tenniscan said, "This doesn't make sense. When we're in charge and there's law and order, our country shouldn't look like future Trouble."

Picklecrat said, "This doesn't make sense to me either. When we're in charge and there's equal opportunity, social justice, and programs to support basic necessities, our country shouldn't look like future Struggle.

Professor said, "Clearly you were expecting better results when your parties ran things. Yet as you can see, without balance and cooperation, it doesn't work."

Hope interrupted them. "The future is not all bad," she said. "Let me show you the future in Thrive. It's quite different. Its peaceful and prosperous."

Then Hope revealed holograms of a day in the life in future Thrive. They were shown newscasts, street scenes, and views across the country. In diners and parks, hospitals and libraries; everything appeared to be calm. People were generally happy and going about normal activities.

"So, what did they do differently?" Hostility asked.

Professor corrected him. "It's not what they did, it's what they will do. I know it seems confusing, but all that we are showing you hasn't happened. For now, this is what the future could bring if things remain on the current path," Professor reminded them.

"Okay, I get it," Hostility said and then she restated her question. "What will they do differently?"

Hope explained, "The need for a functional government is essential. Without it there is chaos and anarchy and that's not freedom. Therefore, people will choose to work together cooperatively. They will develop a plan for their government that is grounded in their common interest of freedom, opportunity, and justice. It will be their duty to work towards the common good, build community, and set the guardrails through a Bill of Rights to amend their Constitution."

"Here's a little guide for you," Professor said, as he handed them future Thrive's Bill of Rights. It began with a preamble:

We the People of Thrive, in order to preserve our Union, preserve Justice, preserve domestic Tranquility, provide for the common Defense, promote general Welfare and secure the Blessings of Liberty to ourselves and our posterity, do ordain and amend this Constitution to ensure a Functional Government.

The politicians and broadcasters read the document.

After a few minutes, Professor broke the silence and asked, "What do you think?" Everyone remained quiet.

"Perhaps it would be better if you could experience it for yourselves," Hope suggested. Professor agreed and then set the ground rules for interaction with people in future Thrive.

Instantly, the group arrived in the small city of Rockwell near the town square. The mystics chose October 10th, which in future Thrive will be a national holiday called Constitution Day.

They arrived just after sunrise. They saw the eager faces of people lining the streets for the parade that was to begin in about 20 minutes. Children clutched flags and bounced on their toes, while adults chatted animatedly as they looked towards the distant sounds of marching bands that were tuning up for the festivities. Street vendors hurriedly arranged their wares which added splashes of color to the festive scene. Balloons bobbed and swayed as the crowd buzzed with excitement.

The area where they arrived was near the mayor's special viewing tent which was positioned at the parade's focal point. The tent was adorned with fluttering banners and ribbons in patriotic hues and included a large grandstand area with views of the procession route. The group was seated at one of the many small tables under the pavilion adjacent to a Lions Club concession stand where they were selling coffee, hot chocolate, and pastries. Patrons huddle around small tables and enjoyed their morning treats. Their laughter blended harmoniously with the festive environment.

The mayor greeted dignitaries with warm smiles and firm handshakes as he walked towards the podium to make a brief commencement speech. He began:

"As your mayor, it is both an honor and a privilege to welcome you to celebrate the 25th Anniversary of Constitution Day." The crowd applauded enthusiastically, then he continued.

"Rockwell is a shining example of our great country Thrive. We cherish the value of unity, fairness, and progress and it is with great pride that I stand before you today to reaffirm our commitment to these principles."

"I am most proud that our citizens are educated on the issues of the day and can come together peacefully every 10 years to participate in our national referendum. It is a tribute to this great country and the core of what this day symbolizes. By letting the people choose our moral path, it frees our government to function as originally envisioned by the drafters of our great Constitution." There was more applause.

"First and foremost, let me emphasize our unwavering dedication to nonpartisan governance. In a time where other countries are still suffering from their great political division, our city and this country stand as a beacon of cooperation and collaboration.

Though I am a member of the Unity party, I can honestly state that I embrace all citizens regardless of their political affiliation: Picklecrat, Tenniscan, Unity or other, on this day and every day.

I applaud all of you as you actively participate in the process for being educated on the issues, and working together to address the needs of our community.

My term is ending soon. And on this 25th Anniversary of Constitution Day, the day that symbolizes the people taking back control of our government, let me reaffirm my continued support for the Bill of Rights that was enacted to safeguard our freedom.

I affirm the value of term limits that ensures fresh perspectives and ideas to continually invigorate our leadership. By embracing change, we foster a culture of innovation that prevents the entrenchment of power.

I affirm our fair voting practices and the eradication of gerrymandering which are fundamental tenets that protect our democracy. Every voice deserves to be heard and every legitimate vote must be counted. In this way our electoral process remains transparent, equitable, and free from manipulation.

I affirm our role in moderating social media. Our approach to online communication is one of tolerance, respect, and empathy. Let us continue to use social media as a platform for constructive dialogue and understanding, rather than a tool for division and anger.

This day is also here to remind us to remain vigilant in our resolve to fight the corrosive effect of unchecked campaign financing and the damage it causes to our democratic process. By limiting campaign contributions and keeping them transparent, we safeguard the integrity of our elections and ensure that the voices of ordinary citizens are not drowned out by the influence of special interests.

Above all else, this day is here to celebrate and encourage the camaraderie and civility of our citizens. This is what truly makes our nation great. It is through your active participation, your dedication to community service, and your unwavering support for one another that our city thrives. Together we are building a brighter future for generations to come.

The crowd enthusiastically applauded the mayor. Then, he led them in the singing of a rousing rendition of Thrive's national anthem and the parade began.

The Bill of Rights

As the mayor walked back to the viewing area, the mystics stopped everything in its place, except for him. They ushered him to the table with the politicians and the broadcasters and kept him in a state where he was unaware that all activity around him was frozen.

Professor said, "We're from out of town, and have come here to talk to you about Thrive's Bill of Rights."

The mayor sat down and said, "Welcome to Rockwell. If it's the Bill of Rights that has your interest, you've certainly picked the right day." Then he asked, "Did you hear my speech?" They all nodded yes. "Good, because I wrote it as a testament to what we've accomplished over the past 25 years. Then he saw Tenniscan reach into his jacket pocket and pulled out the version that Hope had given him.

"I see you have a copy," the mayor said.

"Yes," responded Tenniscan. "Perhaps you could give us some additional context on the ten articles and explain the problems that each was trying to resolve."

"Sure," responded the mayor. The first two Articles addressed *eggselection* and *racket control*. We understood the critical importance of protecting the rights of the minority and avoiding the tyranny of the majority. Yet, these two issues were dominating national politics at the expense of everything else. So, it was determined that these two issues would be settled by national referendum. This did not invalidate laws granting equal protection under the law, nor deny or abridge the right to vote in any manner. Though, on these two issues, voters were allowed to set the general framework for what is legally acceptable and then the states regulate the details."

Every 10 years, the people of Thrive will decide whether *eggselection* should be unlimited; totally banned; or have limits set. And if they vote for setting limits then they will also vote for the scenarios that are minimally and maximally acceptable; such as the term of the egg and whether it involved violence.

Similarly for *racket control* the people will decide if ownership rights to rackets and paddles as weapons should be unlimited; totally banned; or have limits set. And if they vote for setting limits then they will also vote for the scenarios that are minimally and maximally acceptable; such as age, training, registration, and licensing.

The states were then tasked with regulating each of these issues within the parameters set by the national vote.

Hope looked at the politicians and asked, "Do you think tackling the moral rights of *eggselection* and *racket control* by referendum will work?"

Picklecrat was the first to offer an opinion, "I think it's a good thing to allow people to set the framework. And, I agree that the topics of *eggselection* and *racket control* are too dominant and are used as litmus tests for those running for office. It does limit discussion on most everything else. Still, I'm not sure if referendum is the answer, but I'm willing to give it a try."

Tenniscan offered, "For over fifty years politicians have been unable to reach consensus on these issues. So, establishing tolerable limits that the majority supports by referendum might be a good start, even if that means voters hold their noses while doing it."

After a long discussion, it appeared the group was open to the idea and then the mayor moved on to the other Articles.

"The third Article *Term Limits*. We established term limits and age limits for all elected and appointed officials; with a maximum of three Congressional terms; two Senate terms and twenty years of total service."

Snarky said, "Having skilled legislators is important. Having politicians preventing functionality... not so much. So, Term Limits is an easy one for me. Almost everyone favors it. Don't you agree Hostility?" He asked with a grin as he shrugged his shoulders.

Hostility said simply, "Nobody wants career politicians."

The politicians sat quietly as they knew that they had exceeded the new term limits. Still, they reflected on the value of their experience and rationalized that their long service had truly helped the country.

The mayor continued and explained that the fourth Article, *Fair Voting Districts* was designed to eliminate gerrymandering. It established a non-partisan method for drawing the lines to create fair voting districts. This was done by using analytics that included voter population, minority demographics, and party affiliation. The results set reasonable geographic boundaries within each state such as county lines and natural boundaries like rivers and mountains that did not favor one party over the other. They were each aware that when one political party controlled the state government and had the ability to draw the lines without limitations, they did so in a manner that slanted the results to favor their party. It was clear to them that the method in Dire, Struggle and Trouble was skewed. So, there was minimal debate on this topic as it was grounded on the premise of basic fairness.

"The fifth Article was *Voting Integrity* which was critical," the mayor stated, "as without it, we would be like Dire. We saw what was happening there, as people lost faith in the voting process and the civil war that followed. We chose to prevent this from happening on Thrive."

He explained the principles to which Thrive was committed which restored trust in their voting system:

1) that only legal, registered voters could vote; requiring voter ID that was fair and not unreasonably burdensome;

2) that absentee ballots were appropriately controlled and limited to those with legitimate reasons for not voting in person;

3) that voter rolls were kept up to date systematically;

4) that voting was made more accessible by making it a national holiday, adding longer hours and one extra day to limit wait time to less than an hour;

5) that the results were fully auditable with a complete paper trail to validate every vote and that voting occurred a month earlier to provide plenty of time for each state to certify their results; and

6) that it established open primaries; with the top two candidates from each party primary being placed on the final ballot and then utilized ranked choice as a method to determine the winner.

Professor said, "Looks like quite an overhaul, but it seems fair. How has it worked?"

"It was an overhaul" the mayor responded. "Voter turnout increased, and most importantly trust in our voting system was maintained. We credit this article with preventing what happened in Dire and what is happening in Struggle and Trouble."

Hope asked, "Can you explain how ranked choice works, as it's a bit confusing to me?"
"Sure," the mayor answered. "Often there is not a winner who initially gets 50% or more on the first round. When this happens, the candidate with the fewest votes is eliminated with those votes being redistributed based on the second-choice preference. The process of elimination and redistribution of votes continues until

one candidate obtains more than 50%. It has stopped the election of extreme candidates and clearly favored centrist candidates as intended."

Hope smiled as she pictured it working, even on Dire and felt a sense of optimism.

"This approach can work," Professor said. "And it should moderate the two-party system." Then he looked at the politicians and said, "You must agree that it only takes a few extremists to stop everything; whether they're Picklecrats or Tenniscans?"

The politicians looked at him sheepishly and remained quiet as they were fully aware that what he said was the truth.

"Well, the party's over," Snarky said sarcastically. "No pun intended," he added with a slight giggle.

Hostility just laughed, nodding her head from side to side. She knew this would throw a wrench into party dynamics and she was having a moment of private enjoyment as she pictured the impact. After a few more minutes on the subject, the mayor continued.

"One of my favorites is the sixth Article, *Filibusted*. This limits each Senator to one filibuster per 6-year term and three filibusters per calendar year for each registered party. So, folks need to use them wisely," he said with a big smile on his face.

"Seems like a smart idea to me," Hostility interjected. "Filibusters should be limited, like timeouts in sports." The solution was practical and even the politicians couldn't object.

The mayor then discussed the seventh Article *Financial Security*. It was very detailed as it required Congress to pass an annual budget on time; as part of a 6-year plan; that included immigration and asylum targets; and a 10-year outline for a balanced budget.

The mayor said, "The best part of this one is the enforcement if Congress is unsuccessful." He explained that if a budget was not passed on-time it triggers re-election. It would begin with an automatic Continuing Resolution to extend the existing budget for six months and proceeds with the immediate re-election of all House members and 50% of the Senate by random selection; all to be completed within four months.

"That's a great idea," Snarky offered. "Running a multi-trillion-dollar budget month to month is crazy. Do your job, or you're fired! Brilliant," he said with glee.

Hostility agreed, "the idea that the budget is part of a 6-year plan with a path to being balanced in ten years is a good start. And setting targets for immigration makes sense. We need these folks to fit into our economy; they need to support it, so it can support them."

"I don't see this working any better than our current approach," said Picklecrat with a touch of bitterness in his voice.

Tenniscan followed, "We can't even agree on a one-year budget. I can't imagine something this big being completed even once with Picklecrats. And the thought of doing it annually is laughable."

"That's exactly the point," said the mayor firmly. If you guys can't get this done, maybe the next bunch can."

"It requires everyone to work together, and that's really the point," Hope said as she softened the tone of the conversation.
"Still, you can see, the people of Thrive expect their government to function. And it may take a different set of skills. Perhaps you all need more accountants and fewer lawyers," Professor said glancing at the politicians as he added a little humor.

After a while, the Politicians calmed down as they began to understand that things will need to be different. Then, the conversation turned towards the remaining items.

"The eighth Article, *Media Moderation* was the most challenging," the mayor said. "It was apparent that when people limit their access to information from only one source or point of view, there is a serious risk of being misinformed by lies and propaganda. Determining the facts is essential and with the volume of editorial and bias, the truth is typically found in the middle. So, we encouraged people to get their news from a broad range of media. This included broadcast, print and social and we further suggested the need for a variety of sources and viewpoints.

"How did that work out?" Snarky asked.

"We quickly learned that it wasn't enough to sift through all the noise. So, we regulated it. We required that all media companies moderate all information prior to public release including all sponsored ads and recommended content pushed at users."

"We need to regulate big tech as well," Snarky interjected. "We're creating a culture of conspiracy theorists. Whether it's *Fake News* or *Alternate Facts*."

"That's what we did," the mayor responded. "In fact, we required source referencing of all information, transparency on the algorithms used to target recipients and disclosure of any AI or artificial content."

Tenniscan said, "I have some serious reservations on this one as this definitely limits free speech."

The mayor understood his position, though stated, "These are limitations, but they're absolutely necessary. We already place limits on speech. We don't protect fraud, obscenity, defamation and hate speech. So, we asked ourselves, why should we protect lies and distortions that threaten our democracy? We shouldn't. So, we decided to moderate them."

Snarky nodded in agreement. "I agree with the mayor," he said as he glared at Hostility. "Especially given all the conspiracy theories you're pushing. You get your viewers outraged and then it gets amplified exponentially online."

"Give me a break. You're not innocent of all of this. You must not watch your own show," Hostility responded.

Professor interrupted them. "I understand that you claim your shows are only entertainment. Social media companies claim that they are only bulletin boards. Still, you should be responsible for misinformation and the harm it causes. Thrive's decision to moderate it seems reasonable."

Hostility offered, "My issue isn't with moderation, it's with the moderators. Why should we trust these companies to moderate themselves? And how do we regulate them?"

The mayor answered, "We had similar concerns when this was enacted so we added a few twists. First, we broke up the monopolies to foster competition. Then we made it easy for users to leave by requiring interoperability to make information interoperable across platforms.

"What do you mean by interoperable?" Tenniscan asked.

The mayor responded, "Interoperable is where content is more freely exchangeable and useful across multiple platforms. And we added a "right to exit" so users could take their followers with them

Hostility concluded, "So what you're saying is, if you don't trust the moderators of a given platform, interoperability makes it easy to switch, even to a startup and leave them behind. You can take your stuff and your friends anywhere. So, you're not a hostage to one provider."

"You've got it. That's exactly what we did," the mayor responded.

Hostility added, "What worries me is all the foreign meddling. They push their agendas and social media companies get paid to do it."

"We addressed that too," the mayor said. "We made them divest foreign ownership as we determined that the data and algorithms that influence users are issues of national security."

The politicians had a side conversation on the topic and it was clear that they were aligned. They did not want foreign governments to be able to access our data and influence domestic policy and especially our elections. Hope overheard their conversation and nodded in agreement. Then she opened her arms for emphasis and said to the group, "Remember, we've shown you the future where unmoderated lies and unlimited money leads to civil war. You need to fight this with everything you've got because it's tearing you apart."

The mayor reacted to Hope's comment and continued. "Of course, we also recognized the influence of money as someone is paying social media companies to push this information to users and it's more like advertising than news. So, beyond moderation and foreign divestiture, we regulated lobbying and political advertisement through the ninth article *Campaign Finance Reform*."

Then he explained that this article prohibited all dark money from corporations and non-profits; limited donation amounts to $5,000; and set maximum spending levels by the candidates and their respective surrogates by office; $2M for Congress; $5M for Senate and $100M for President.

"You're on to something there," Picklecrat said. "Do you realize how much money it takes to get elected? It's obscene. From the minute you run for office, it's all about money. And it doesn't stop there. After the election, it gets worse. There's an obsession to constantly raise money. And, heaven forbid if you cross any of those special interests, you get *Primaried*."
"Then why aren't you doing anything to fix it?" Professor asked.

"Because it's bigger than just one Congressman. It's the whole system. Money is fuel and the two-party-system runs on it," Picklecrat answered.

"That's exactly why Thrive included it in the Bill of Rights; we needed to fix our political system and money was what drove it," the mayor stated.

Then the mayor looked at his watch and said he had to get back to the festivities. "But before I go, I'll simply tell you that the tenth article *Civility* was the most fundamental. This is where we put *civil* back in *civilization* by giving tax breaks for participating in non-partisan civic organizations and even joining sports leagues. That's the secret to Rockwell, civility and an expectation of general decency. Which is something I'm sure you've discovered and where the other countries have lost their way."

And with that, the mayor said goodbye to the group and rejoined the festivities without missing a beat.

Civility

Hope said, "Everything we've discussed with the mayor is a good start. But, without Civility the rest doesn't matter."

Professor nodded and said, "And in Dire they've lost their way, because they've lost their civility. They've lost their decency."

"True," Hope agreed and continued, "In Dire, everything becomes an argument as everyone is angry as intended by the media. They tell people that they need to be outraged. But it wasn't always this way. You all need to reflect and understand why?"

Snarky then asked, "Are you suggesting that people are simply no longer good? That we need *good people training*?"

"No. That's not what I'm saying. You're still good. It's the environment that's changed. You all live in a world of media hype. The solution is simple. You need to remove yourselves from the hysteria, unplug, and spend time working on common causes. You need to be Braver Angels and that needs to be encouraged."

"So that's where the tax credits come in?" Picklecrat asked.

"Yes," Hope answered.

"Is there no end to what you Picklecrats are willing to spend our money on? Tenniscan stated. "Do we really need to pay people to go bowling?"

"Yes, and to play softball, join the Lions Club and work at the local food bank," Hope answered firmly.

"Can't you just waive your magic wand and make things better?" Hostility asked.

"That's not how it works. You need to learn how to get along and work together again. You need to be reminded of all your shared interests. And that those interests are woven into the fabric of your country. And, I know you can do this. That's why I believe everything will be okay," Hope said optimistically.

Professor offered, "Of course, we'll leave some of those Braver Angels behind to help, but it's really up to you. Now that you've seen the future are you willing to try?"

Heads nodded signaling their willingness.

Then Hope and Professor smiled and with a wave they were gone.

A discussion on its meaning

After Marty finished the story, he sensed the group was energized. Several offered their agreement with the solution the story presented and wanted to talk about it some more. They began to discuss it as they walked towards their cars in the parking lot.

"My friend gave me a box of these books to hand out, so, I'll make sure you each get a copy, Marty said.

Susan said, "How about after next month's event, we get together to talk about this some more? They all agreed.

"I'll bring the beer," Steve offered. There were many smiles.

"Sounds like a plan," Marty said.

A month had passed. The run was another big success and afterwards, they met as planned and sat at the picnic tables. Steve brought out a large white cooler that was full of beer and sodas, plenty for the ten friends that had assembled. "Bars open to everyone, whether you're a Tenniscan or a Picklecrat," he joked.

"Funny," Terrance said.

At first, they discussed the charity run and how well it had gone. They congratulated Susan for her effort and a few offered thoughts on what could be done differently next year.

Then Marty asked the group, "Well, what did you think of my friend's story?"

"Wait a minute," John interrupted. "Before we get started. Let's set some ground rules. First, I understand that Bill and Tom have patched things up and have agreed to be on their best behavior. They each have promised me that they won't get into it again. Still, let's all do our best not to attack each other."

Everyone was a bit nervous as they looked around and made eye contact with others. They seemed to reach a silent agreement to do their best to avoid major argument.

Steve then offered, "I really think your friend's on to something. He presented many of the areas we're struggling with and did it in an insightful manner."

"Exactly," Susan said. "Using pickleball and tennis was very creative as it captured the fight we're seeing between Democrats and Republicans. And the framework he used lowers the temperature on the competing passions we see on these issues."

"He also showed us that our government is stuck and needs our help," John said.

The group then discussed each of the articles. Steve was quick to call out the political parties. "The story reveals the constant battle between Democrats and Republicans. But we're witnessing this at another level. Extremists have shut things down. So, I support the story's premise that we need to elect more centrists."

Don agreed with Steve and added, "But, the parties are rigging the districts and they're rigging the vote."

"Are you saying that they're cheating?" Susan asked.

"I really don't know. I'm saying that people believe there's cheating and that's the problem. Perception is reality. And with more swing states and closer elections, even the appearance of cheating is harmful. And the story showed us that when you don't trust the voting process, bad things happen."

"What if creating distrust in our voting is their strategy?" Bill asked.

"I'd say the strategy worked," John answered.
"Either way, I want voter ID," Tom said.

Then Tom noticed Bill's soured expression and then asked him, "What's wrong with wanting only legal voters to vote?"

"Nothing," Bill answered. "So long as it's reasonable. And at the same time, what's wrong with making voting more accessible by adding more locations and extending the voting periods so folks in the city aren't waiting in lines for hours? Or that the working poor can even vote?"

"Nothing, I guess," Tom replied. "Unless, it's for too many days."

"It's another partisan issue," Steve interjected. "Republicans believe Democrats want to make it easier for *illegals* to vote because they vote Democratic. Democrats believe that Republicans want to make it harder for minorities and the working poor to vote because it limits Democratic votes."

Susan, always the voice of reason, added, "You would think that both Democrats and Republicans should support having the highest legal turnout possible. And, I'm emphasizing legal," she said while making air quotes. "And the way to do this is with stronger voter ID and extended voting periods."

Bill sniped, "And when people trust the results, the Vice President can ceremonially count them." His comment raised a few eyes as he subtly referenced the last election.

"Of course, that issue wasn't settled," Susan responded not missing a beat. "What happens in an election where the incumbent loses and the Vice President simply refuses to certify the count? She asked. "It could happen, it almost did."

John, who was an attorney, tried to answer her question. "Each state needs to certify their results based upon the Rule of Law and someone needs to close this loop, whether that's Congress, the Supreme Court, or by referendum. In any case, like you Bill, I believe the transfer of power needs to be orderly and remain ceremonial."

With that comment, there was silence, as everybody tried to avoid argument by rehashing the events of January 6th.

Tom quickly stepped in and said, "And that's the beauty of this story, it's designed to get people talking and consider things sensibly. I wish Bill and I had read this book earlier," he joked.

"Clearly, I'll keep it civil," Bill replied with a conciliatory look on his face.

"As a CPA, I liked the suggestion that we elect more accountants and fewer lawyers," Don quipped. "No offense, John."

"None taken, Don." It's funny and true," John said as they all laughed.

Linda agreed and said, "The call for civility resonated with me. Is it too much to ask people to be decent? To tone things down? To stop labeling friends as enemies?"

She got more animated as she spoke and continued, "I want people to drop the torches and pitchforks and stop threatening public servants. Whether that's volunteers at the polls, teachers, police, or elected officials. They are our neighbors. The bullying and the threats need to stop. It's not right, and it's not even practical as these are important jobs that people won't fill in the future. Something's got to change."

"I think it's too late, the civil war has begun," Don declared.

"There's nothing civil about it," Marty responded.

Steve said, "Isn't that the moral of the story? Civility. We need to get along better and to rebuild trust by simply being together face to face."

"You're right," Marty said, "It's hard to hate people up close."

Steve said, "I think we have three choices, civil war, compromise, or divorce."

"Really and if we chose divorce, how would you divide things?" Don asked.

"Red states go red. Blue states go blue. And, purple states are divided by county."

Like "Brexit?" Marty asked.

"Yes, an American exit."

"Funny," Marty said.

"I'm not joking," Steve continued. "Give them five years to establish geographic borders, carve up the debt, share the cost of defense and establish the rules for Social Security and Medicare tied to state residency to avoid senior migration. No shots fired."

"Civil war is not the answer, even if no shots are fired," John exclaimed. "The winners in an American civil war are our enemies. The military has a name for it. It's called PSYOPS. Psychological Operations, where the goal is to disrupt and confuse the enemy's leadership to make it ineffective. Sound familiar? Don't trust the Voting System. Don't trust the President. Don't trust Congress. Don't trust the Supreme Court. Don't trust the Judicial System. Don't trust Policemen. Don't trust Teachers. Don't trust each other. See where this goes?"

Marty nodded and said, "I don't think we're in a civil war yet, but there are too many people who are disenfranchised and have deep-rooted anger. Whether that's folks fighting for equality and social justice, or those who want to protect their individual freedoms and not be burdened to make up for the sins of the past."

"But did they need to turn to violence?" Bill asked referring to the events of January 6th. "To me that exposed how fragile things are."

John said, "January 6th was a toxic moment, and a wakeup call. And it's just as wrong as the violence Tom referenced in the BLM protests. Still, our government needs to function and we need to set the guardrails."

Susan, always the optimist chimed in, "I think we're at a turning point," she predicted, "In the long run you'll see our resilience. Americans are durable and democracy is durable, but we've got to do the work."

"How?" John challenged. "By playing well with others?"

"Yes." Susan answered. "We need to rebuild faith in each other; one American at a time. Things may seem dire right now, but we can prevent The Great Pickleball Wars."

"You've got my vote," Marty said.

Then the friends reflected on the story for a while longer and continued their discussion on solving America's problems.

"So, what's next?" John asked.

"Well, there are organizations out there working these issues," Marty said. "One of them is called *Braver Angels*. Their mission is to bring Americans together to bridge the partisan divide. You may want to see how you can get involved."

"Thanks," John said. "But what I meant was it's getting late and I have to go. And, I was thinking perhaps we should all get together again from time to time, rather than waiting for next year's run."

"What do you have in mind?"

"How about we go bowling?"

They all laughed. Then they thanked Marty for sparking the conversation and Steve for bringing the drinks.

"Remember, get involved and share the story," Marty instructed.

And with that, they said their goodbyes and headed off with a new challenge

Resources:

Here's how you can download the Photer App:
https://photer.net/download.php or scan the QR code

Here's more information on the Braver Angels mission:
https://braverangels.org

Here's information on the National Constitution Center:
https://constitutioncenter.org/

Pew Research Center re-election statistics:
https://www.pewresearch.org

Here is an overview of Thrive's Bill of Rights.

- Articles 1 & 2 – "Moral Rights" required that the Laws for *eggstruction* and *racket control* be settled by national referendum every 10 years.

- Article 3 – "Term Limits" established term limits and age limits for all elected and appointed officials; with a maximum of three Congressional terms; two Senate terms with a maximum total service of 18 years.

- Article 4 – "Fair Voting Districts" eliminated gerrymandering and established a non-partisan standard methodology to create fair voting districts with reasonable geographic boundaries set within each state; consistent with their voter population, minority demographics and party affiliation.

- Article 5 – "Voting Integrity" required voter ID, open primaries; top two candidates from each party on the ballot; ranked choice with centrist method; controlled absentee ballots; responsible voter rolls, extended voting days, hours, and locations; and disputes settled timely by state Rule of Law; leading to a ceremonial Congressional count for Presidential elections.

- Article 6 – "Filibusted" limited each Senator to one filibuster per 6-year term; and each registered Party to two filibusters each calendar year.

- Article 7 – "Financial Security" required Congress to pass an annual budget on time; as part of a 6-year plan; that included annual immigration and asylum targets; and a 10-year outline for a balanced budget. If unsuccessful, there was an automatic 6-month Continuing Resolution and immediate re-election of all house members and 50% of the Senate by random selection; to be completed within 4 months.

- Article 8 – "Media Moderation" required that all media companies moderate and source reference all information prior to public release including all sponsored ads and recommended content they pushed; transparency on the algorithms used to target recipients and disclosure of any AI or artificial content; and established liability and related fines. Social media companies are required to make content interoperable across platforms with users given the right to exit with their followers. It also set a maximum market share for these companies at 15% and required the break-up of monopolies to ensure competition

- Article 9 – "Campaign Finance Reform" prohibited all dark money from corporations and non-profits; limited donation amounts to $5,000; and set maximum spending levels by office; $2M for Congress; $5M for Senate and $100M for President.

- Article 10 – "Civility" put the "civil" back in civilization by providing tax breaks for participating in non-partisan civic organizations and group recreation like the Lions Club, Kawanis and sports league

Made in the USA
Monee, IL
14 July 2024

61736590R00052